DIGGING FOR T

The Message of The Cross Today

Edited by
Derek J. Balsdon

A MET Publication
In partnership with

The **Leaders of Worship**
and **Preachers Trust**

Published on behalf of MET by

ISBN 978 0 86071 792 8

First Edition published in United Kingdom 2019.

Copyright 2019 MET

All rights reserved.
No part of this publication may be reproduced, stored in a retrieval system, or transmitted, in any form or by any means, electronic, mechanical, photocopying, recording or otherwise, without the prior written permission of the publishers.

British Library Cataloguing in Publication Data.
A catalogue record for this book is available from the British Library.

CONTENTS

	Page
INTRODUCTION *Derek J. Balsdon*	1
1: THE PRIORITIES FOR PREACHERS *Jonathan Lamb*	3
2: THE DYNAMICS OF BIBLE EXPOSITION *Jonathan Lamb*	11
3: PREACHING AND APOLOGETICS *Amy Orr-Ewing*	28
4: THE EXPOSITORY PREACHING OF 'CHRIST CRUCIFIED' *Derek J. Tidball*	45

Methodist Evangelicals Together

is the largest independent organization in British Methodism today, a renewal movement uniting and representing evangelicals at every level within our denomination.

Our three core purposes are:
- **ADVOCATING:** Promoting and representing evangelicalism within Methodism, and Wesleyan evangelicalism within the wider evangelical world.
- **EQUIPPING:** Providing resources through publications, conferences and our website for evangelicals within British Methodism.
- **SUPPORTING:** Offering pastoral support and advice to evangelicals, who can often feel isolated within Methodism and face particular pressures.

MET is a fellowship for every Methodist who shares our desire to:
- Uphold the authority of Scripture
- Seek Spiritual Renewal
- Pray for Revival
- Spread Scriptural holiness
- Emphasise the centrality of the Cross

MET promotes partnership in the Gospel to proclaim Jesus as Lord. Our partners include:
- Cliff College
- ECG
- LWPT
- Share Jesus International
- Inspire Network

Join MET and partner with us to:
- *Network with evangelical Methodists in prayer and action.*
- *Add your voice to 1700 others on key issues at all levels of the Methodist Church and beyond.*
- *Participate in national and local events.*
- *Receive the MET Connexion Magazine.*

Find us at: www.methodistevangelicals.org.uk

Or write to us
c/o Moorleys Print & Publishing, 23 Park Road, Ilkeston, Derbys DE7 5DA
who will pass on your valued enquiry

INTRODUCTION

Derek J. Balsdon

Development Worker, Methodist Evangelicals Together

These contributions to our Digging for Treasure resources for expository preaching take us deeper into the ancient written word of God and bring forth a life-giving message of the cross for this twenty-first century. In his sermon, Jonathan Lamb shares some important priorities for preachers through expounding 2 Corinthians 4:1-6. In his chapter on Nehemiah 8:1-12, he uses Ezra the priest as an example of one who gave a clear explanation and application of God's written word. He reminds us that effective preaching is not just dependent on the work of the preacher and on the work of the Holy Spirit; it also requires that the congregation are expecting to hear God speak to them, and to draw them deeper into God's grace, which comes through the cross.

Amy Orr-Ewing uses her skills as an apologist to demonstrate the effectiveness of using questions to help people explore issues of life and faith, following the example of the Bible itself. The questions that were asked by Jesus, and asked of Jesus, automatically take us to the one who lovingly gave his life upon the cross for those with whom we communicate. Asking questions and exploring answers helps to open minds and hearts to God's love and grace. Within our preaching ministries, and also within our conversations with people, we should not be afraid to ask and explore these questions in this twenty-first century.

Since the early church era, the cross has been the primary symbol of Christianity. Derek Tidball writes of how preaching the cross is still one of the distinguishing marks of evangelical

Christianity. He expounds the many-sided wonder of the cross through looking at the Gospels, the Letters, in later theology and in the contemporary church. His penultimate paragraph is a wonderful summary of what we can experience from the cross, through the death and resurrection of Jesus Christ. Through our proclaiming Christ crucified, both in preaching and in conversation, may more people experience his life-changing grace today.

It is our hope and prayer that this publication will help preachers, Bible study leaders and individuals delve deeper into the rich treasures within the Bible, to *'taste and see that the Lord is good'* (Psalm 34:8). Expounding the written word of God still enables people to experience the living word of God, Jesus Christ, and his life-transforming love and power.

THE PRIORITIES FOR PREACHERS

2 CORINTHIANS 4:1-6

Jonathan Lamb

Minister at large of Keswick Ministries
and as a Vice President for IFES

This morning I travelled into London on the M40, and I'm very thankful that it was a clear run. But on weekdays the situation is often very different. As thousands of commuters drive into London, it is common for there to be traffic jams as you reach the M25. The other day I was sitting in the traffic, along with many other commuters, and as we were waiting I looked across to a field, to a message which had been painted on a boundary fence by a graffiti artist. It was a question for all of us commuting into London: *Why do I do this every day?*

It is a good question for us too. What are our priorities in Christian service? Why do we do what we do? What really matters for us as preachers? In Acts 6 the apostles were very aware of the danger of being distracted from the priority tasks of the ministry of the Word and prayer and it is wise for us to review regularly the priorities which shape our ministry too.

Paul's defence in 2 Corinthians helps us to see the key priorities in his life. He faced many temptations to compromise his message and his methods. He was being criticized for a range of issues by a group of rivals in Corinth who had a very different view of leadership and apostleship. They challenged his authority, they invaded his territory and claimed credit for his efforts, and they mocked his abilities as a preacher. By contrast, they displayed more dramatic signs of spirituality, they had more impressive rhetoric, and had far superior knowledge.

So this short passage provides us with an insight into what really matters in Christian ministry, the priorities that should shape our preaching of the Word.

1. Knowing God's call - vv1-2

'Therefore, since through God's mercy we have this ministry, we do not lose heart.' (v1)

The first encouragement for Paul was the fact that his ministry arose from God's call. Verse 1 refers to the ministry of the new covenant, about which he has been speaking in chapter 3, and we can see that Paul viewed his task of proclaiming the gospel as the central ingredient in this ministry of the new covenant. He could put up with almost any difficulty because he knew it was God who had called him. He was an ambassador, as he says in the next chapter; he had been given a message and a mandate by God himself.

This God-centredness is seen in chapter 2:16. *'Who is equal to this task?'* he asks. How can we possibly serve amongst those who are perishing and those who are being saved? He makes it clear in 2:17 – it is because *'we are like those sent from God'* and he affirms the same truth in chapter 5:18-19 *'God gave us the ministry of reconciliation'*.

Many of us feel exactly the same as Paul: we look at the challenges in our work, or in our society, or we look at our own feelings of frailty, and like Paul we ask: *however am I going to do it?* But I am sure you find it to be true: we can put up with a great deal if we know who it is who has called us and what it is that God has called us to do.

The sense of accountability to the God who called him is reinforced in verse 2. '*We commend ourselves to everyone's conscience in the sight of God'*. One recurring feature in 2 Corinthians is his appeal to God as his witness. I find Paul's emphasis here very challenging. There is nothing casual about his ministry. He knows he stands before God, he is accountable to him -and so are we. We are first and foremost serving the God who has called us; we are carrying out all of our work *'in the sight of God'*.

So first, our ministry is the result of God's call. It is not dependent on our resources, but on God's mercy and faithfulness toward us.

2. Explaining God's Word - v2

'We have renounced secret and shameful ways; we do not use deception, nor do we distort the word of God. On the contrary, by setting forth the truth plainly, we commend ourselves to everyone's conscience in the sight of God.'

Next, Paul underlines his determination to be faithful to the message. He stresses a key priority: we are not to distort the Word of God but present its truth plainly. This is the great privilege and responsibility of every preacher: to ensure that God's Word is central.

To *'set forth'* the truth means an open declaration, a full disclosure of the truth. It is the opposite of deception. It means *'to show your hand'*. It is like the conjuror or the magician at a circus, who rolls up his sleeves - no rabbits! So Paul insists, we are holding nothing back, we are proclaiming faithfully the whole counsel of God.

Look at how he describes his ministry in 2:17 *'Unlike so many, we do not peddle the word of God for profit. On the contrary, in Christ we speak before God with sincerity, as those sent from God.'*

It is possible that these preachers were similar to the occult cults of the day, salesmen who were marketing a new and mysterious religious product. Maybe the word pedlar originally referred to those who watered down wine for sale in the market. They were guilty of distorting the product, the message, but they did not care. They were salesmen whose sole motive was personal profit. We are not sure what this might have represented, but maybe it was a gospel which majored on strength not weakness, a message which promised triumph not suffering, a gospel which paraded glory not the cross.

So Paul affirms his commitment to a faithful, clear, open declaration of the truth. And this discourse is an important opportunity to ask if this is a priority for us too.

3.   Proclaiming God's Son - v5

'For what we preach is not ourselves but Jesus Christ as Lord.'

Not long ago an article appeared in a Christian magazine which suggested that, at least in some parts of the Western world, there was emerging a consumerist attitude in the church. It was described as a 'McChurch mentality', which was pushing Christian leaders and pastors to market themselves and their church in an almost competitive spirit. It suggested that congregations approached sermons in much the same way as they approached fast food restaurants. Today, McDonalds; tomorrow, Burger King.

In Paul's day there certainly was a problem with personality cults and a drive towards showmanship. In chapter 10 Paul quotes his critics: *'In person he is unimpressive and his speaking amounts to nothing.'* And he confesses in 11:6, *'I may not be a trained speaker'*.

His rivals in Corinth were clearly very concerned about image, about projecting themselves, their eloquence and their rhetorical skill. Paul is not afraid to confront that directly in verse 5 of our passage: *'we do not preach ourselves'*. We are not projecting our personalities. As he says in 5:12 *'we are not trying to commend ourselves to you again'* – we are not trying to build our own power base.

And he had already said this very directly in his first letter. *'When I came to you I did not come with eloquence or human wisdom ….. For I resolved to know nothing while I was with you except Jesus Christ and him crucified.'* (1 Cor 2:1-4)

Here in 2 Corinthians 4, it's the same. *'We do not preach ourselves, but Jesus Christ as Lord.'* So in 1 Corinthians – Jesus Christ and him crucified; and here in 2 Corinthians - Jesus Christ as Lord. That was the essential message that Paul wished to proclaim. Jesus Christ as Saviour and Lord and he wanted nothing to get in the way of that message. That was the authoritative proclamation that really mattered.

I am sure you will feel the challenge of this. To proclaim Christ Jesus as Saviour and Lord is an increasing challenge, isn't it? In the context of today's pluralism it is not uncommon for Christians to be asked why they are so arrogant as to claim that the gospel is for every person and every culture. These verses help us to respond with conviction to this basic question. Paul's focus was Jesus Christ. He saw that the great priority of his life was to preach Jesus Christ as Saviour and Lord - and so it must be for us.

4. Trusting God's power - vv3-6

In response to his priorities, Paul's critics would probably have come forward with another accusation. His preaching was ineffective, they said. Their approach, their techniques, would produce a far bigger response. It is true – preaching God's Word, proclaiming Christ, is a tough job, often with limited results. So Paul responds in verses 3 and 4.

'And even if our gospel is veiled, it is veiled to those who are perishing. The god of this age has blinded the minds of unbelievers, so that they cannot see the light of the gospel that displays the glory of Christ, who is the image of God.'

These verses remind us of two certainties, two realities in our work.

First, spiritual blindness. It is possible that with the use of the words 'veil' and 'glory' Paul is making the same contrast that he made in chapter 3, where he said that the Jewish people didn't really understand their own scriptures. There was a veil over their hearts and minds and the Holy Spirit was the only one who can remove it.

In the same way, now in chapter 4 he says it is true of all men and women. We know this to be the case - there are many who are spiritually resistant. In the parable of the sower Jesus says much the same. *'The devil comes and takes away the word so they can't believe and be saved.'* So that is why our ministry of preaching and teaching needs also to be accompanied by our urgent prayer for those who hear. But that leads us to Paul's second certainty:

Second, spiritual illumination. *'For God, who said, 'Let light shine out of darkness', made his light shine in our hearts to* *give us the light of the knowledge of God's glory displayed in the face of Christ' (v6).*

As we do our part in proclaiming Jesus Christ as Lord, then we have the assurance of God's illuminating work in the hearts and minds of people. Just as in his work of creation, by his Spirit God shines his light into the hearts of people to reveal the truth about Jesus. And as we've seen, the whole passage is very Christo-centric. The light that dispels the darkness of the human heart is found in the face of Jesus Christ. Paul demonstrates that the only way to know God is to know Jesus Christ, who is the image of God, the one who reveals God's glory to us.

So it is only by preaching Christ and only by the illuminating power of his Spirit that men and women are taken out of the kingdom of darkness and brought into the kingdom of light. Just as Paul is realistic about the god of this age, so he is totally optimistic about the power of the message to impact people's lives.

When I was at school I spoke with a friend almost every week about the Christian faith. He was much more intelligent than me, and he won every argument. It went on month after month. And by the end of our school career, he still had not become a Christian. Then we both went to different universities, and in his first week he walked into a Christian meeting on the campus, and became a Christian. When I received the news I have to confess that my first thought was – *that's so unfair! All those years of trying to present the gospel!* But then I realised the truth which Isaiah had recorded. Do you remember his description of the water cycle? The rain falls, it waters the earth, the seed produces fruit, and the water evaporates back to heaven. *'So is my word'*, the Lord says. *'It will not return to me empty, but will accomplish what I desire and achieve the purpose for which I sent it'* (Isaiah 55:10,11).

Our priority is to trust God's power – to be faithful in proclaiming Christ and praying for the illuminating power of God. The seed is the Word, and the Kingdom will advance only as that word of the gospel is proclaimed and by the Spirit provokes a response in the hearts and minds of those who are ready to hear and receive it. *'The gospel is the power of God to salvation to everyone who believes.'*

Let's notice once again the force of verse 1 – *'we do not lose heart'*. One of the greatest enemies in Christian service is discouragement; we often face the temptation to give up. In this passage we are urged not to lose heart, but to live and work by these fundamental priorities:

Knowing God's call
Explaining God's Word
Proclaiming God's Son
Trusting God's power

'Therefore, since through God's mercy we have this ministry, we do not lose heart.'

THE DYNAMICS OF BIBLE EXPOSITION

NEHEMIAH 8:1-12

Jonathan Lamb

Minister at large of Keswick Ministries
and as a Vice President for IFES

Some years ago J B Phillips was working on a paraphrase of the New Testament and explained that the experience was similar to working on the mains electricity of a house, but doing so with the electricity still switched on. It was an electric experience! The book was 'live', it was powerful and energising. As Luther put it, *'The Bible is alive – it has hands and grabs hold of me, it has feet and runs after me.'*

The Bible is full of dynamic descriptions of the Word. Jeremiah said that God's Word was like fire in his bones, or like a hammer that breaks a rock in pieces. Paul described it as the sword of the Spirit. The idea is repeated in Hebrews 4: *'living and active, sharper than any two-edged sword'* (Hebrews 4:12). Jesus said that the Word was the seed which produced a wonderful harvest.

There is the intriguing story in Luke 24, when two disciples were walking home to Emmaus after the dramatic events of Jesus' crucifixion in Jerusalem. They didn't recognise Jesus, but he deliberately chose not to reveal himself, other than through the Bible.

'And beginning with Moses and all the prophets, he explained to them what was said in all the scriptures concerning himself' (Luke 24:27).

In other words, it was through scripture that they encountered the living Christ. The reason why our churches are committed to listen to, explain and understand God's Word is because we believe it has the same dynamic impact today. It transforms understandings, and attitudes; it changes lives; it draws us into a living relationship with God.

There is a great example of this dynamic Word in action in the story of Nehemiah 8. When you read the narrative (vv 1-12), it is good to ask: 'What are the elements in this story which demonstrate what is happening when the Bible is opened as it should be?'

There are three key themes to look at as we consider the core elements of Bible exposition:

Firstly: **The Word of God and the heart of preaching**

The opening verse of chapter 8 introduces us to a new section of the book, all to do with the spiritual restoration of God's people. The building of the walls is now over, but the true foundation for the restored community will be God's Word. There are two features of the text which demonstrate that Ezra and Nehemiah saw the Word as the foundation for all that was to follow.

i) Its centrality
The seventh month for God's people was a month of great religious festivity, and their first act was to call for the book. Verse 1 describes the grassroots desire that the law should be read: *'All the people assembled before the Water Gate. They told Ezra the scribe to bring out the Book of the Law of Moses, which the Lord had commanded for Israel'.*

In verse 3 the law commanded the attention of everyone -*'all the people listened attentively'.*

It retained its central place, day after day, right through to the end of the month. The Word of God represented the foundation articles, the new constitution of the people of God. For a nation seeking its identity and shaping its programme of restoration, the Word of God mattered. It was central. There is even something symbolic in the fact that it was not read in the Temple but, according to verse 3, *'He read it aloud from daybreak till noon as he faced the square before the Water gate'.*

ii) Its authority
Here it is simply to note the emphasis of verse 1: *'They told Ezra the scribe to bring out the Book of the Law of Moses, which the Lord had commanded for Israel.'* Its human authorship is acknowledged on several occasions - the reading was from the books of Moses. But its divine authority is emphasised - the law of God, the revelation given by him. The law was 'teaching' or instruction from God himself. Without this sense of divine authority it would simply be the veneration of a book and that is the vital perspective for our own understanding of scripture too. There is a wonderful explanation of this in 1 Thessalonians, where Paul describes the way in which the believers received the gospel.

'We thank God continually because, when you received the word of God, which you heard from us, you accepted it not as the word of men, but as it actually is, the word of God which is at work in you who believe.' (1 Thessalonians 2:13)

There are two significant themes here. Firstly, *its authority*: it is *'the word of God'*. This is very emphatic in the way in which Paul wrote it. The message of the apostles is authoritative because it originates with God himself. Secondly, *its power*: *'which is at work in you who believe'*. It is powerful precisely because it is God's Word. We shouldn't drive a wedge between the written word and the living God who speaks that word. By

God's Spirit it is powerful, life giving, life transforming. It 'goes on working'. It is not simply propositions, distant and cold, but a dynamic Word that, by the power of the Spirit, turns us round to serve God and shapes the way in which we are to live. That is the foundation for our authority, conviction and passion as those called to preach.

Some implications:

1. *Bible exposition must be centred on God's Word*

I spoke some while ago with a pastor in one of the Central Asian Republics. He said: 'I write my sermon and then look for a Bible passage to support it'! It is a surprisingly common strategy. But this is to use the Bible as a peg on which to hang our thoughts. If we do this we are not allowing the Bible to speak. But as we have seen from Nehemiah, the Word must be centre stage. So we must *'preach on the passage, the whole passage and nothing but the passage'*, as David Day has expressed it. There are two important reasons why this should be so.

First, *the Bible passage establishes our authority*. Preaching is not authoritative because of our personality, our academic study, or our communication skills, but because of the authority of the God who speaks that word.

Second, *the Bible passage defines and limits the message*. It gives us the subject and shapes all we have to say. It is the architect's plan.

2. *Bible exposition must be immersed in God's Word*

If preaching is to have this Biblical dynamic, then those of us who preach need to be wholeheartedly committed to immersing ourselves in scripture - there are no short cuts. There are many other things that will crowd in to exclude the study, prayer and meditation which good preaching requires. I have no doubt at all that it is a constant challenge. The apostles in the New Testament soon discovered that many things distracted them from the priority of the Word and prayer (Acts 6:1-7), and that they needed to take action to ensure that first things were first.

The same commitment is underlined in Paul's encouragements in the Pastoral Epistles, *'give attention to the public reading of scripture, to preaching, to teaching… Put these things into practice, devote yourself to them, so that all may see your progress. Pay close attention to yourself and to your teaching…'* (1 Tim. 4:11-16).

3.   Bible exposition must open up God's Word

When we look at the New Testament words for preaching, it is clear that they point towards one issue: preaching is not announcing our own words in our authority, but proclaiming God's Word with his authority. There are four word groups which help us understand the nature of preaching. The most common word group means to *declare as a herald*. Preaching is to proclaim the message which is given with the authority of the God who sends us. The message is not generated by the messenger, but it is given by God himself. The second relates to *announcing the good news*. It is not used exclusively in the task of evangelism, though it includes this. Again, it is God's good news, not ours. The third group of words relates to the task of *witnessing or testifying to the facts* and the fourth word, which is often translated *'teaching'*, is to lay out the facts as God has revealed them.

Notice the emphasis is on the 'given-ness' of the message. We are to proclaim the *Word of the Lord*.

Further, if we look at Paul's instructions to Timothy we see how insistent he was that pastoral ministry involves faithful, urgent, proclamation of that Word. So Paul presses home the point – our task is to proclaim the Bible. Nothing else will do, for nothing else reveals God's purposes, nothing else has such transforming power.

Good Biblical preaching arises from an attitude of mind, a submissive approach to the scriptures and to the God who has spoken that Word. The style in which this is done or the structure which is used will vary greatly according to our culture, our tradition and our personality. But the core commitment is universal.

Some challenges:

i) Addressing Biblical illiteracy and the loss of confidence in the Bible
The church survey, *'Taking the Pulse'*, set up by the Bible Society and the EA, revealed a loss of confidence in the Bible and therefore a loss of its centrality. One of the questions was: *'Do secularists like Richard Dawkins affect our confidence in the Bible?'*, and a quarter of church leaders admitted that the attack of militant atheism affected their confidence. 40% of church goers felt their confidence in the Bible was undermined by this trend. There are other troubling statistics: 70% of church goers indicated that they didn't read the Bible outside church events or on a regular basis.

We know that this generation has little or no Biblical understanding – not even at the most basic. Don Carson speaks about Biblical illiteracy: *'We are not simply writing fresh data on the blank hard drives of their minds; we are required to help them erase certain files ... that clash irremediably with the truth of scripture that we are trying to write on to their minds.'*

ii) Restoring the centrality of the Bible in church life
The marginalisation of preaching is just one aspect of the marginalisation of the Bible. So we need to work hard to restore its central place - in our homes, our church life, our small groups and in our preaching. Deuteronomy 6 reminds us that our love for God will be expressed by our determination to bring his Word into the centre of our life, our families and our Christian communities:

'These commandments that I give you today are to be upon your hearts. Impress them on your children. Talk about them when you sit at home and when you walk along the road, when you lie down and when you get up. Tie them as symbols on your hands and bind them on your foreheads. Write them on the doorframes of your homes and on your gates' (Deuteronomy 6:6-9).

Secondly: The teacher and the work of preaching

Next we turn to Ezra the priest and his team of helpers. There are several significant features of their service that day in Jerusalem.

i) Making it accessible
The text is extremely clear at this point. If God's Word was to be the foundation for their families, their day-to-day living and their society, then it had to be clear, it had to be accessible to everyone.

v1 *'All the people assembled as one man'*. Ezra read before the assembly *'which was made up of men and women and all who were able to understand'* (v2, repeated in v3); then *'all the people could see him'* (v5). So there was every attempt made to ensure that everyone had access to God's Word. But there is more...

ii) Making it clear
The account shows us the stress placed on understanding - not only the texts we've mentioned –*'all who were able to understand'* (v2), which must have meant men, women and children – but also the emphasis on making the content of the law clear. So we have verse 8: *'giving the meaning so that the people could understand what was being read.'*

The reason for the people's response is recorded in verse 12: *'because they now understood the words that had been made known to them'.*

The fact that the reading of the law was not just for priests or Levites, and that Ezra chose the city centre rather than the temple, strengthens the sense that the law needed to be heard and understood by everyone. It was – and is – God's Word for all.

iii) Working together
Verse 4 demonstrates that Ezra chose a group of others to help him with the reading, and verses 7 and 8 show that teams helped with the interpretation and explanation.

In some cultures the preacher or the pastor can sometimes come across as the professional, the expert. But the important task with which we are charged is not only to teach, but through our handling of the Bible also to help others to understand how to enjoy scripture. In that sense, we are not just providing a good meal, we are aiming to help others know how to cook, how to prepare a meal for themselves. We need to find ways to engage others in this task.

Implications for preachers

4. Bible exposition must be focussed

As we have seen, Ezra and Nehemiah were concerned that everyone should understand. Biblical preaching must focus on this urgent priority too. It begins, of course, with the preacher working hard on the Bible passage. I like the way Eugene Peterson expresses it, *'Exegesis is loving God enough to stop and listen carefully to what he says.'*

But it is more than this. For effective preaching, there is also one important aspect to understanding the passage: to understand its *primary message*. What is the big idea of this passage, as we often say? What is its melodic line? What is the *heartbeat* – the key idea which is pumping the blood round, the life-giving force of this passage of scripture?

In order to understand the passage and to communicate its meaning to our congregation it is essential to have discovered this big idea, the main theme which will dominate our message. For me, this is the most important part of my preparation. Unless I am clear about this, I will not be able to preach with conviction and with passion. It is this which is central to Bible exposition. It is exposing the fundamental meaning of this passage, opening up its force and power, showing people how it applies to them and urging them to accept it and respond to it. That is preaching with focus.

5. Bible exposition must be clear

Ezra and his team worked hard at the task of making the reading of the scriptures clear. We have seen the different ways in which they did this, doubtless involving translation, interpretation, discussion and explanation. The Biblical preacher must do the same. Sadly, we know this is not always the case. Sometimes there is a fair amount of fog in the pulpit. Some preachers leave people less clear after the sermon than they were before it.

Related to this, we will help our listeners have a better understanding of what we are saying if we are clear in the way in which we present our message. Some form of structure is nearly always helpful. A clear structure helps the preacher organise his thoughts and present them in persuasive and memorable ways and a good clear structure helps the listener to concentrate and focus on the Bible passage, and to remember the key point later.

The goal is exactly the same as it was for Ezra's team of helpers who *'helped the people to understand ... They gave the sense, so that the people understood the reading'* (vv7-8). That is what clear preaching does.

6.   Bible exposition must be relevant

As well as making the text of the Bible accessible and clear, we must engage not only with scripture but also with our listeners. So we work hard to present the material not only in a way that can be grasped, but also in ways that resonate with their situation. As we prepare to preach, we must spend time not only thinking about *what we are preaching about*, but also thinking about *who we are preaching to*.

If we are going to communicate the dynamic force of any Bible passage, then our application of it must connect with the needs we perceive in our congregation, or the challenges of our culture, or the circumstances of our hearers. The great preachers of the Bible – the prophets, the apostles, Jesus himself – were all concerned to contextualise the message in ways which directly addressed their hearers. But we should note that application *first of all* arises from the questions and the challenges and the comfort of the Bible passage itself.

Some challenges

i) Restoring confidence in preaching
It is true that preaching these days doesn't get a good press. Pulpits in the West are seen as platforms for self-appointed bullies. Some dictionary definitions don't help: 'to preach' is *'to discourse on moral or religious topics, especially in a tiresome manner'*. But it seems there is also a hunger, and in some countries it is especially amongst the young. A recent survey about church life made reference to a 15-year-old who was asked, *'what would your church lose if it lost the sermon?'* and he replied, *'The congregation'*. He was right. The survey indicated that young people are definitely not anti-preaching, but keen to understand and to live the truth. There is a welcome seriousness in the rising generation, for which we must thank God and to which we must respond.

ii) Strengthening training
It is happening, but much more needs to be done, especially through non-formal approaches. I often recommend the use of small preachers' groups – in the work of Langham Preaching these are called preachers' clubs, and there are thousands of them around the world. This can be a group from different churches, or a group within one church. I know of preachers in a Colombian city who meet together to prepare from the same passage, and then preach that same passage in their different churches on Sunday. Many of us have been a member of a preachers' club in our own church – with the regular preachers and the youth workers and some home group leaders, perhaps meeting over breakfast on Saturday, working together to understand and apply the passage. Often preachers are lonely, and we need to work together, just as they did in Nehemiah's day.

Finally, we come to the third main element of the story in Nehemiah 8. The Word was being read and also carefully explained. But as we have said, the Word of God is dynamic - it has an effect. Something was happening to the hearers.

Thirdly: **The congregation and the purpose of preaching**

We read not only about the role of the teachers, but also the active participation of the congregation.

i) They were expectant:
They were eager to hear the Word. To begin with, we see in v1 that the initiative was with the people who called on Ezra to bring out the Book. Jim Packer makes the surprising suggestion that it must have been like the crowd at a rock concert: *'Imagine an impatient audience as a rock concert picking up the chant, 'We want Ezra, we want Ezra', saying it over and over, louder and louder, and you get some idea of the feelings being expressed'*.

That same sense of eagerness and expectancy is expressed in verse 3: *'all the people listened attentively'*; and verse 5, as the people stood up when the Book was opened, and verse 13: *'everyone gathered to give attention to the words of the law.'* It reminds us too that there is little to be gained from reading the Bible without such expectancy. Jesus' own ministry was frustrated when there was no expectancy on the part of his hearers - he began to teach in the synagogue and he was met with cynicism and incredulity. Expectant faith is the soil in which God's Word will bear fruit, and that is a lesson throughout our Christian life.

ii) They were serious:
Here is a further sign of their spiritual hunger. They were ready to cope with all kinds of inconvenience in order to hear this Word. Here the Water Gate congregation stood from daybreak

to noon (v3) - for at least 5 hours, without a coffee-break in sight - because they longed to hear and understand what God had to say to them.

And then we read in verse 6: *'Ezra praised the Lord, the great God; and all the people lifted their hands and responded, Amen! Amen! Then they bowed down and worshipped the Lord with their faces to the ground.'* Maybe there is something to learn from the attitude of the people in Jerusalem that day: a longing for God to speak as they lifted up their hands; an attitude of reverence and respect as they bowed with their faces to the ground. Perhaps these attitudes are pre-requisites to understanding God's Word and coming into his presence. Indeed, the verse is important in reminding us that we don't venerate the book as such: its purpose is to bring us into the presence of its author - the Lord, the great God.

Nehemiah 8 demonstrates one important element of true teaching – it should bring us into God's presence. It mediates an encounter not merely with truth, but with God himself.

iii) They were obedient:
Finally we notice the result. The people experienced God's Word in such a way that it called for a response at a variety of levels. Verse 9 shows the initial response: *'For all the people had been weeping as they listened to the words of the Law'*. Their first hearing of the law provoked within the people a sense of contrition as they realised that their lives had failed to match up to the standards which God had set. But intriguingly, Ezra and Nehemiah move quickly to set that failure within the wider context of God's purposes for his people and, with the encouragement of the leaders, the people went to celebrate, to eat and drink *'with great joy'* (v12). They had come to realise that it was God's desire to bless them, and they had come to see that from all that had been

read - *'they now understood the words that had been made known to them'* (v12).

The rest of chapters 8 and 9 demonstrate the impact of the Word on the people. The prayer moves towards an expression of covenant renewal. They were ready for action. They wanted to live their lives in conformity with God's Word, to demonstrate in their community that they belonged to him.

That is the significance of the sequence of these chapters. It is hearing God's Word, celebrating God's goodness, knowing God's grace and then obeying God's laws. It is truth in action. As we have already seen, truth is dynamic and life changing. We are called to *do the truth* not simply to believe it.

Implications for preachers

7.   Bible exposition must call for change

Effective preaching calls for a response. All preaching must be transformational preaching. We know that Jesus left no room for neutrality or boredom when he preached. And in his record of various sermons preached in the book of Acts, Luke often describes how the people reacted, not with passivity, but with joyful acceptance, or alarm, or amazement, or even antagonism.

Preaching is not just to inform or instruct but it seeks to produce transformation of life. As Paul said about the Romans, *'But thanks be to God that you …. have become obedient from the heart to the form of teaching to which you were entrusted' (Romans 6:17)*. The aim is to make God's Word clear so that, by the Holy Spirit, people understand it in their own situation and then obey it – it has the purpose of transformation.

8.   Bible exposition must engage the listener

Jesus was particularly insistent that his audience truly heard what he was saying: *'Let anyone with ears to hear listen!'* That seems to have been one of his characteristic sayings (Mark 4:9, 23; Luke 8:8).

Hearers need help in listening, and we should learn from the response of God's people throughout scripture – expecting an encounter with God, ready to respond to his Word and open to be changed by its power. Preaching should be a dynamic and a divine event.

As Luther said: *'I just threw the Bible into the congregation and the word did the work.'*

9.   Bible exposition must proclaim God's grace in Christ

The story in Nehemiah 8 demonstrates how the reading of the book of the law exposed the sin of the people (so they wept), but pointed them to the mercy of God (so they rejoiced). Then in Nehemiah 9 the people confessed their sin, enjoyed God's grace, and renewed their commitment to him. Biblical preaching must always do the same. It must be grace-filled. And for us, standing now in the light of the New Testament, to preach grace we must preach Christ.

Luther used to describe scripture as the cradle in which we will find the baby. Its purpose is not to draw attention to itself, but to the person of Jesus. For the scriptures, both Old and New Testaments, point to Jesus Christ. We see in 2 Corinthians 4 that Paul stresses the twin priorities of explaining the Word clearly and presenting Christ faithfully. Christ-centred preaching is the fundamental priority.

All preaching must be biblical preaching. And biblical preaching will be gospel-centred, empowered by the Holy Spirit's energies, and will call for radical change.

Some challenges:

i) The need for double listening
There is an urgent need for application. Time doesn't allow us to develop this theme, but it means listening to scripture and also listening to the challenges in our world. We need to understand both the pastoral needs within our congregation, and also the uncertainties and confusion of our culture.

ii) The need for integrity
Ezra has been central in the Nehemiah story. What made him such a remarkable figure? It is summed up in a pithy expression found in Ezra 7:10, *'For Ezra had devoted himself to the study and observance of the Law of the LORD, and to teaching its decrees and laws in Israel.'*

The one dominant verb – *devoted* – describes his commitment to three things, described by the verbs: *study, observe, teach*. He had set his heart and mind fully to that essential sequence – his own study of the truth led to his *doing* the truth, which only then led to his teaching the truth.

Here we come to a fundamental element in the dynamics of Bible exposition: *the word must be embodied* in the life of the preacher. There is sometimes a loss of credibility in preaching because of the way in which we fail to live the life. As I have engaged in seminars in different continents over the years, the comments have always been the same. In Hong Kong I was told that Chinese pastors preach well, but behave terribly at home; in Africa, most countries appeal that any training event for pastors must include a session on being a godly husband and acting faithfully in marriage and family life; and in Asia, here is what one wife wrote: *'I would like to know more about Langham Preaching, because not only does my husband preach better, he is a much nicer person!'*

Preachers not only need to heed the usual advice of practising what we preach: perhaps we should only *'preach what we practise'*. I realise that to do so will drastically reduce the length and variety of my sermons, but it is at the heart of integrity and essential for the authentic preaching of God's Word.

These then are the dynamics of God's Word at work. They demonstrate why Bible exposition is used by God's Spirit the world over, whatever the culture and whatever the personality of the preacher. True Biblical preaching is a divine and therefore a dynamic event, as the scriptures are opened and lives are transformed.

[A more extensive treatment of these themes, based on the Nehemiah story, is to be found in Jonathan Lamb's book, *'Preaching Matters: encountering the Living God'*, IVP, 2014, ISBN: 978-1-78359-149-7]

PREACHING AND APOLOGETICS

Amy Orr-Ewing

Director for Oxford Christian Centre of Apologetics
and Senior Vice-President, RZIM

The focus of this talk is on preaching to the outsider using apologetics. Apologetics sounds like something very academic, abstract or clever, but it comes from the Greek word *apologia*, which just meant 'a reasonable defence'. If you were on trial in court, your lawyer would say an 'apologia' on your behalf. So it means a reasoned defence or a persuasive speech about something that you really believe in, to try to persuade people to come around to your point of view.

When we talk in the church about apologetics, it really means the same thing: talking persuasively about the Christian faith. The most famous passage is in 1 Peter 3:15, where Peter tells Christians to *'Always be prepared to give an answer to everyone who asks you to give the reason for the hope that you have. But do this with gentleness and respect'*. The word that we translate as 'answer' is the Greek word *apologia*.

Background

Several years ago, my father began to ask, 'When I get to 65 and look back on my life, what will it have all been about? Is there something more?' A few weeks after beginning to ask that question, my father walked into the back of a lecture theatre where a Christian apologist was speaking about the resurrection of Jesus Christ. My dad did not hear the whole message, but as he walked through, the only sentence he heard was 'The only reason that you should believe in Christianity is because it is actually true.' My father was intrigued by that statement, because to him religion and truth were opposing categories – it was an oxymoron to put those two categories together. Religion was about fantasy, delusion and culture, but it certainly couldn't be about truth. That intrigued him, but he didn't think about it much more. Then one night, a few months after that, he was marking some exam papers in his study, and the rest of us were all in bed. It was quite late at night, and he had an extraordinary experience where his whole life flashed before him, scenario after scenario, from childhood through to the present day. During this vision, which took some time, he saw the scenarios from his life replayed. He saw the choices he had made, the things he had thought and said, and he saw the reactions to those things on the face of Jesus Christ. I've asked him many times, 'How did you know it was Jesus, given your upbringing?' and he said, 'I don't know how. I knew, I just knew that this was Jesus.' And then at the end of the experience, he found himself on his knees and he saw Christ on the cross, and the only words that he knew from the Bible – perhaps from school or a friend – were *'Lord I believe, help my unbelief'* (Mark 9:24). And he then he got up off the floor, as a Christian.

He went in and woke my mother up, and said, 'Jane, the most incredible and fantastic thing has just happened. I've become a Christian.' She was less than excited by this development and rolled over and went back to sleep. Over the next few days my father thought, 'I wonder what Christians do?' So he went to a shop and bought a Bible, and started to read from Genesis. He then thought, 'How can I meet other people who like Jesus and read the Bible, and may go to church?' He hadn't stepped into a church as an adult, and said to his wife, 'I am too embarrassed to go to church by myself. Will you please come with me?' She knew that her husband was intelligent and so she came up with a plan to reconvert him from his Christian faith. So she said, 'I will come to church with you, but only if

it is an Anglican church', as she thought that once he experiences that, he will be cured for life and will be fine.
They went through the Yellow Pages, and picked an Anglican church that was near them, and they walked into the church that Sunday morning. They didn't know it, but they had picked a Bible-believing church. It was filled with young people like themselves. The sermon started and the preaching was from Romans chapter 1, where it describes the wrath of God, his justice, his reaction to sin and evil and violence, and the conviction of the Holy Spirit that comes into the world. My father sat there as he heard the scriptures describe what he had just experienced in his study: a conviction of sin, which caused him to weep as he heard this sermon. His wife was absolutely furious, as she thought 'How dare anybody say that there is a God who will judge and hold us accountable, for the choices that we have made?'

Over the next six months, my parents argued a lot, and my father tried to evangelise my mother. He would sit her down and say 'Jane, the thing is, you are in darkness and you need to come into the light. You are lost – you are like a fluffy sheep, which needs to be found.' But it didn't really work, as sharing faith within families can often be tense and difficult.

My father wrote letters to all sorts of people in his life, not only to tell them what had happened to him (to share this good news), but also to say sorry for things that he had done to them. He even wrote to his atheist father. There was one colleague in particular that he wanted to share his faith with, so he wrote and invited him to dinner. When the friend walked in, he said 'I was so happy to receive your letter, because six months before this happened to you, something similar happened to me. I became a Christian. In my church, I was told to read the Bible, and also to write a list of people that we are going to commit to pray for, and to pray for them every day, and you are on my list. But before I got to share about Jesus with you, you were sharing about Jesus with me!' My mother was thinking, 'Oh no. I thought we were going to have a nice evening tonight, and these guys are Christians now!' The friend turned to my mother and said, 'I've read from the letter that you are not a Christian.' He did something brilliant in that moment, he asked her a question: 'Why not?' So, she began to share about why she wasn't a Christian and through that conversation the friend was able to address the issues. She then knelt down on our sitting room floor, and turned her life over to Jesus Christ.

That moment, when both of my parents had become followers of Christ, was a moment of revolution for our family, because within a few months, my parents had sold everything, including their house, and heard a call from God to pursue an evangelistic ministry. So I grew up in a home where Jesus was real. He had appeared to my father and he had invaded the life of my mother and did a very dramatic miracle in her life that night. And we saw God at work in amazing ways in our home, with people becoming Christians, getting healed and experiencing extraordinary things. It was also a place where I was encouraged to raise questions and to deal with doubt by finding answers. I then went on to study theology at Oxford, which was an interesting and quite hostile context within which to speak about the Christian faith. I had to try to take the questions and objections that some of the brilliant minds in the world had thrown at God and the Bible, and see if there were answers.

So really apologetics is about connecting with people – their questions, their world, the authorities or sources they might listen to – and using those connection points in preaching. Apologetics (connecting with people) is something that all witnessing Christians should be doing every day.

Expectations in preaching

It is a privilege to be able to share a few thoughts about preaching that I have picked up along the way that might be helpful. We all bring different experiences, voices and expectations to a preaching ministry, but expectation is where I would like to start. What do you expect when you preach? What do you imagine you are doing?

> Bonhoeffer took preaching seriously. For him a sermon was nothing less than the very word of God, a place where God would speak to his people. Bonhoeffer wanted to impress this idea on his ordinands, to help them see that preaching was not merely an intellectual exercise. Like prayer or meditation on a scriptural text, it was an opportunity to hear from heaven, and for the preacher, it was a holy privilege to be the vessel through whom God would speak. Like the incarnation, it was a place of revelation, where Christ came into this world from outside it.[1]

Preaching is an encounter

It is about Christ's presence in HIS word - it is pretty awesome. Bonhoeffer wrote:

> The proclaimed word has its origin in the incarnation of Jesus Christ. It neither originates from the truth once perceived nor from personal experience. It is not the reproduction of a specific set of feelings... The proclaimed word is the incarnate Christ himself,... the thing itself. The preached Christ is both the Historical One and the Present One... The proclaimed word is not a medium of expression for something else, something lies behind it, but rather is the Christ himself walking through his congregation as the word.[2]

After a sermon from an anointed preacher, you know that God is real. He is there and it shakes us.

Preaching is a calling

Paul wrote *'Woe to me if I do not preach the gospel!'* (1 Corinthians 9:16). We don't chose preaching, it choses us. Ravi Zacharias was asked about calling and he was told not to waste people's time giving people blessed thoughts from the pulpit, but only to do so if he had a sense of awe, preparation and calling.

Preaching as part of the spiritual battle
For me a controlling scripture is:

> *Then I heard a loud voice in heaven say: 'Now have come the salvation and the power and the kingdom of our God, and the authority of his Messiah. For the accuser of our brothers and sisters, who accuses them before our God day and night, has been hurled down. They overcame him by the blood of the Lamb and the by the word of their testimony; they did not love their lives so much as to shrink from death…'* (Revelation 12:10-11)

'Overcoming' suggests that a battle is to be fought and won. Preaching is engaging in the spiritual battle. It is unleashing God's objective truth AND the application – our own testimony – the two together.

Preaching with the breath of the spirit
Preaching is the word proclaimed with the breath of the Spirit: the authority, glory and presence of Christ. Not stirred up by shouting, emotional manipulation or gimmicks, but words spoken by a human touched by God himself.

The word is powerful, raw, edgy, surprising, humorous, intellectually stretching, practical, thrilling, shocking, disturbing, encouraging and comforting. It is never to be shallow or merely self-help truisms.

Practical Application: preaching with and through questions

Questions are unbelievably effective in apologetics and in preaching. We can ask:

- 'Have you ever wondered...?'
- 'I want to ask you a question tonight that I truly believe is worth your attention: Who do you say Jesus is?'
- 'Have you ever wondered if there could be a God, who created all this?'
- 'Have you come to a conclusion about the meaning of life? Are you open to the possibility that there is a God who loves you, who has come for you and who offers you life?'

Questions help us in sensitive areas not to be overbearing. We can ask, 'Might you consider this claim of Jesus?' or 'Are you willing to invite him in to help you with your sorrow/broken heart and deliver you from darkness to rescue you?'

In the gospels, there are many occasions when Jesus asked questions, as part of his preaching ministry. He asked 157 questions and all of them are brilliant. How many sermons have you heard on a question that Jesus asked? We are going to look at a few questions which Jesus asked and see how they can help us in our interactions. What do we say to friends who hold opposing views that they are highly committed to? Perhaps they are highly sceptical, disinterested, successful or wealthy and don't see a need for the Christian faith. A question can often help in the circumstance, as it can do many things.

1. A question can intrigue and connect to a desire for meaning

'*What do you want?*' (John 1:38). This is the first thing that Jesus Christ says in John's Gospel and is therefore very, very important. It is the first time that the Son of God, who John has told us is the *logos*, the source of information, DNA, the first mover of the uncreated, creator of space, and time, and history, and rationality and people. John tells us that the *logos* takes flesh and dwells among us and this is the first question that is asked. Wow! This question is the opener to the whole of the Gospel. Jesus Christ is probing into the very deepest desires and questions of existence, of the human heart. What is it that you want? What is the meaning of life for you? What is its purpose?

Their response was so inadequate, and yet Jesus is so gracious towards them. A question can intrigue, and can stir in the hearts, of even the most hardened person who thinks, 'I don't need God, I am not interested in religion.'

Oliver Sachs, who is not a Christian, but is a great writer in the field of psychology, said this about human beings:

> For all of us have a basic, intuitive feeling that once we *were* whole and well; at ease, at peace, at home in the world; totally united with the grounds of our being; and then we lost this primal, happy, innocent state, and fell into our present sickness and suffering.[3]

He goes on to say, 'We had something of infinite beauty and preciousness – and we have lost it; we spend our lives searching for what we have lost...'[3] This is the guy who wrote the book *Awakenings*, a brilliant man describing the human condition, and he says, 'Every human being that is born is marked by that search for what we have lost in some far-gone distant past.' He could be describing Genesis. What Jesus does here, and what you and I need to learn how to do, is to ask questions that intrigue people and connect them with that desire for meaning and purpose.

A while ago I was at a party with a friend who, on the surface has everything. She is beautiful, has loads of friendships, loads of money, she has three fantastic children and she doesn't need to work. As we were talking, I just asked her a very innocuous question – not even thinking about this – about what she was looking forward to in the next six months. She knew about the vision for our church, and she broke down in tears and said 'I can see that you and Frog [Amy's husband] have purpose in your life and that you are so happy in pursuing that vision, that purpose, but I haven't found mine yet. I am still looking for it. Can you help me?' Wow! That is what Jesus Christ does, when He walks into the room and he begins to move amongst people. He is able, through us, to ask those questions that intrigue people and connect them with a deep desire for meaning.

2. A question can help to get someone thinking
Thinking is not the enemy of truth. In the charismatic church thinking is sometimes seen as the enemy of faith. I have even heard preachers saying, 'Don't think about why some people are not healed, just focus your mind on healing.' That is not what we see in the Bible at all. Thinking is not the enemy of God. God is the *logos*. God is the source of thought and of information. God is that metaphysical reference point for why we can think at all. The great philosopher, Alvin Plantinga, who is one of the foremost Christian minds in the world, has built one of his most brilliant arguments for the existence of God on the fact that there is such a thing as thought. If you are a materialist, you can't understand it, as there is no reference for even describing thought.

What we see is that asking questions can help people to start thinking. In our apathetic Western context, it is not just that people don't like Christianity, or that they don't like church, they just don't even think about it. It is not even on their radar. That is where my parents were, as never in a million years would they have gone to church. There are millions of people like that in our country. What happens when Jesus Christ encounters that kind of person? If we begin to ask questions, he is able, through us, to help that person start thinking about the possibility that there is a God. We can live in a way that intrigues people, but we can help by asking them things.

So asking a question gets people to think, and we see a great example of Jesus doing this in Luke 18:18. A man comes to Jesus and he says, '*Good teacher, what must I do to inherit eternal life?*' Philosophers love this kind of question. Are there absolutes? Do good and evil exist? What is goodness? Is there such a thing as a God? Can you even define goodness without God? I have only been asked this kind of thing two or three times in my life. It is rare that someone you meet will want to know how to become a Christian and I am armed at that point with Nicky Gumbel's book, *Why Jesus?* It is brilliant, because it is really easy to remember, as the way to become a Christian is just to say sorry, thank you, and please. That is the way to become a Christian and inherit eternal life.

But in Luke 18:18, Jesus doesn't provide an answer, but comes back with a question instead, which gets the man thinking. The question is this: '*Why do you call me good?*' He then goes on to say that '*No-one is good-except God alone.*' By asking the question he got the man to think 'You are coming to me saying I am good, but there is no one good except God. So are you saying that I am God? And if you are saying that I am God and that I am good, are you going to do what I say, when I answer your question?' Now I have probably taken ten sentences to do what Jesus does in one question. 'Why do you call me good?' He gets the man thinking. We need to do this desperately, and we need to do this with people who don't believe. We need to do this with people who are aggressive in their belief that God does not exist. We need to do this with people who are living the life of pleasure and who on the surface of things are really happy.

3. A question can bring the focus onto Jesus
It is quite easy in apologetics to find ourselves getting involved in all kinds of conversations. Conversations about science and origins, rationality and thought, language, other faiths and suffering. But what a question can do is to help us bring the focus onto Jesus. In John 2:4, Jesus asks his mum a brilliant question. I love the telling of this story (the Wedding in Cana). I love it, because you can read it and just imagine the dynamic between this mum and her son when the wine has run out and the servants are really worried and are rushing around. The mother of Jesus just says to the servants, '*Do whatever he tells you.*' And she goes up to Jesus and says, '*They have no more wine.*' And Jesus asks her a question, '*Why do you involve me?*' Imagine how many times sons say that to their mothers. 'Why are you involving me?' It raises the question of why Jesus is important. It brings the focus on to him, which is a really important thing to do.

4. A question can define the issue
We can get ourselves tied up in knots or going down cul-de-sacs when we debate people about different issues and questions. But sometimes what we need to do in a situation like that is to ask a question that helps to define the issue. Jesus does it in Matthew 22:15-22, when he is asked about whether they should pay taxes to Caesar or not. I often do this in a context with somebody who is very anti-religion, in order to redefine the issue. I want to help that person see that when we are talking about the Christian faith, it is not a religion, but we are talking about relationship. So we need to redefine the issue.

A few years ago, my friend, Dr Elaine Storkey, a great philosopher and sociologist, was rushing to get to a train to get to a talk that she had to give. She just got inside as the doors of the train were beginning to shut, and sat down in the last available seat going back to London. She found herself sitting next to a lady in her sixties. It was quite a full carriage and it was a typical English situation, when no-one was saying a word. Some people were reading newspapers and there was total silence. The woman next to her, turned to her and began to bluster away. She said, 'Well, I don't know about you, but I can't wait to get back to London. I've just been at my granddaughter's confirmation and I'm absolutely appalled that anyone in my family would get confirmed.' Everyone in the train hid behind their newspapers thinking, 'Please don't let that woman start talking to me'. The woman continued: 'I thought I had brought my daughter up, and hopefully my granddaughter, to be rational. What are they doing colluding with the patriarchal institution of the church? It's absolutely appalling.' My friend said, 'That is interesting,' thinking inside that she didn't really want to get into an argument or debate, so would just let her have her say. The woman continued: 'What do you think about it?'

My friend, knowing what reaction she would produce if she answered that questions immediately said, 'Well, let me ask you a question. What would it take to make you consider the possibility that there is a God? To even be open to that? You have told me of your hostility to the church and your anger about all this patriarchy. What would it take?' And the woman said, 'Well, it would have to be something pretty spectacular.' And my friend said, 'How about if God sent you somebody to tell you that he loves you.' The woman said, 'Well, that would be a start.' By this point some of the newspapers were shaking, as some people were laughing. And my friend said, 'God has sent me onto this train to sit next to you. I'm a Christian. I'm a sociologist. I'm a philosopher, but first and foremost I am a

Christian. God has sent me onto this train to tell you that he loves you.' The woman looked at her, absolutely staggered. They carried on talking and she broke down in tears. It turned out that she had recently been going through a crisis, and lying on her bed late at night and had said to God, 'If you are there? I don't believe that you are, but if you are there, please reveal yourself to me.' A question can define the issue. This is not religion. This is relationship, and in a hostile context we often need to redefine the issue.

5. A question can demonstrate empathy for people
Jesus does this in John 11:34, when his friend Lazarus had died. I don't know if you have been in the situation where you have a friend, who has lost a very close loved one and they are going through extraordinary grief and agony. And one of the things that happens as you grieve is that people don't know what to say to you, and they start to avoid you. And you then have to bear the double agony: not just of the grief, but also the feeling that your friends have abandoned you, because they just don't have the words. What does Jesus Christ do when his friend Lazarus has died? This is a complex situation. You remember that Mary is thinking, 'If you had been here, this wouldn't have happened' How many of us have felt that? 'God, where were you, when I was suffering?' Mary articulates it. It is interesting how the New Testament does not shy away from the difficult questions. Suffering is a reality that is not denied by the Bible. And that question of 'Where is God in the context of suffering?' is on almost every page of the New Testament and the Old Testament. What does Jesus do? He does all sorts of things – and ultimately, he raises Lazarus from the dead – but one of the things that he does, which all of us can do, is ask a question. It is a question that reveals his empathy and his love. He asks, 'Where have you laid him?'

A simple question to a friend who is grieving can be amazing. One of my friends was going through the horrible grief of having very suddenly lost her husband in a violent accident. As I was talking to her, I was asking her about the funeral. The death had happened abroad and she was having to get his body back, and she was going through horrendous trauma. I asked her about the funeral and where they were going to bury him. It was an opportunity for her to just speak about her grief, to talk with me and to process some of what was happening. A question can be a way of expressing empathy.

6. A question can help reveal motives

Jesus asked a really weird question in John 5:6, when he talked to someone who was incredibly ill. This man was paralysed and was lying by a pool that had healing powers but was unable to get into it. Jesus approached him and asked, *'Do you want to get well?'* This was a question that went to the very heart of his motives. A question like this can be very powerful as it can unlock people and help them to understand their desires. Do I want this to be true or not to be true? What is it that I want?

Once, I was speaking in Washington DC and I was invited to go onto Capitol Hill and to speak to a group of staffers from the Congress and the Senate. They laid on a lunch and said, 'We want you to come and speak on the subject "Is Christianity a failed hope? Is Christianity a failure?"' In the context of America, where you have culture wars and violent disagreement between the right and the left, Christianity is very much associated with the right. So this was a hot topic. Before I went there they said to me, 'Well, we are planning this lunch. We have never had more than a hundred show up to one of these, so we think we might get fifty people, but we have sent out an email to everyone who works on the Hill as a staffer in an office of a Congressman or a Senator, and we will just see what happens.'

The night before the event I got a text message saying that they had received 319 RSVPs and they needed to completely revamp the lunch order. I walked into this room, next to the debating chamber, with incredible paintings on the ceiling, and I was to speak from the podium where Bill Clinton and Colin Powell had spoken the week before. I was addressing a group of predominantly young people who were not believers about whether or not Christianity had failed their culture. It struck me that that question was an honest question that cut people to the heart. They were genuinely intrigued and they wanted to come and to ask questions. They were from both sides of the House and some of them were hostile, but others were not. And I found that as I talked to the young people afterwards – many of whom were completely switched off the church – it was the motive that was the most important thing for them. Were they prepared to lay aside their distaste for what they perceived Christianity to be, in order to investigate whether it was actually true, and to see whether what they had seen or experienced was an aberration, and not the reality? Where was the motive? They wanted it *not* to be true, but were they prepared to answer the claims of Christ and see some of the historical evidences, to see some of the philosophical defences of the Christian faith? It was absolutely amazing to see what God did that day. A question can expose motive.

7. A question can open up frank discussion of barriers to belief
This is again something that we don't need to be afraid of. In John 8:46 Jesus said, *'If I am telling the truth, why don't you believe me?'* Now on the face of it, that is a very odd question. Of course if someone believes something is true, they are going to believe it, aren't they? Well, as we often see and know, there are many people in our lives, in this world who may be persuaded of the intellectual case for Christianity, but don't want to believe it. There are other issues at play - barriers to belief, like a moral issue or question or some kind of personal struggle. I find this happening quite a lot in university contexts where we might go and do a freelance talk about the Christian

faith, and half the philosophy department will come and then everybody else will come. Afterwards they have the opportunity to ask questions in an open Q and A, and there will often be a sense of the Holy Spirit moving very powerfully, even in the heart of some of the most aggressive people. And this question needs to be asked, 'If you believe this is true, why won't you take this step and now follow Jesus, what are the barriers to belief?'

So a question can open up a frank conversation, a discussion, of some of those barriers. If we don't know how to ask questions, we are going to be rubbish at talking to people. We all know people who never ask questions, and we may not necessarily like them much, because they just come and talk about themselves. A conversation needs questions.

An illustration

As we ask questions of others, and encourage them to ask questions, we also need to be able to have a go at answering some of their questions and to be able to share illustrations or examples that might help people think through the issues.

The Bible's response to the question of 'Why does God allow suffering?', for example, is rooted in free will. It talks of a good God creating a good world and specifically making creatures who have the capacity to love. But for love to exist, freedom must also exist.

I remember, as a teenager growing up in Birmingham, that I became friends with a girl whose parents were trying to force her into a marriage with someone she did not know. She was 15 and she had every reason to be afraid. A relative of hers had been in the same position a year earlier and had tried to run away, but had been knocked down by a car in the street, dragged home and forcibly taken out of the country to marry. No one had seen her or heard from her again. My friend at 15 knew she didn't want that – she wanted to love and be loved. She felt that being forced into a legal partnership by her parents with someone she did not know and what would happen to her in that situation was the antithesis of love. She believed that the love she was capable of giving and receiving could not be compelled by another – and, fortunately, her friends succeeded in helping her get to a safe house.

Describing this real-life situation is a way of opening up a discussion on a much bigger question: is true love possible without it being freely offered and received? No, it isn't and we all know that is the case. Genesis tells us that God, who is love, made a world in which love is possible, but that also means a world in which there is freedom and humans can use that freedom to do harm, as well as to love.

Conclusion

Ultimately, apologetics should always bring us to the cross by connecting the experiences of the real world with the truth of the gospel. Often the bridge between the two are questions. Questions about our culture, and questions that Jesus himself modelled and asked.

So, as you preach the gospel, let me encourage you to preach for encounter. Preach as one called. Preach in the spiritual battle. Preach with the breath of God's Spirit and preach with and through questions.

Endnotes

[1] Eric Metaxas, *Bonhoeffer: Pastor, Martyr, Prophet, Spy,* Nashville, Tennessee: Thomas Nelson, 2011, p. 272.
[2] Dietrich Bonhoeffer, *Worldly Preaching: Lectures on Homiletics,* New York: Crossroads, 1991, p. 128.
[3] Oliver Sachs, *Awakenings,* London: Pan Macmillan, 1991, p. 29.

THE EXPOSITORY PREACHING OF 'CHRIST CRUCIFIED'

Derek J. Tidball

Author, theologian and Bible teacher

When Paul wrote to the Corinthians, the apostle simply summed up his ministry in the words, *'we preach Christ crucified'* (1 Corinthians 1:23). He was manifestly aware of contemporary discussions and able to engage in them and mount an adequate case for the gospel as Acts 17, among other texts, demonstrates. In synagogues he sought to prove how the Old Testament promises led to Christ, were able to demolish counter-arguments and were able to contend clearly for the faith. But for all the breadth of his knowledge and range of his teaching he ensured that he was never side-tracked into secondary debates and kept his eye clearly on the focus of Christ crucified.

The preaching of the cross is one of the distinguishing marks of evangelicalism. So much so that the Quaker John Bright complained, 'The atonement, always the atonement! Have they (the evangelicals) nothing else to say?'[1] In my experience they have plenty else to say! And, if anything, today they are in danger of marginalising the message of the cross, as huge attention is paid to and emotion invested in other issues. But the cross is our defining characteristic and we need to call each other back to preaching that which is at the heart of our faith rather than at its circumference.

The cross was central to John Wesley: 'The only remedy for "the loathsome leprosy of sin" is to be found at the cross.'

---

[1] Cited in David Bebbington, *Evangelicalism in Modern Britain, A History from the 1730s-1980s,* London: Unwin Hyman, 1989, p. 14.

'Here,' wrote Skevington Wood, 'is the heart of Wesley's gospel and the final clue to its effectiveness. No evangelism will succeed which does not set the Cross in the centre.'[2]

Is there not a danger, it may be asked, that emphasising the cross will lead us to preach a monotonously repetitive message or a shallow mantra? No. The cross is at one and the same time the simplest way to understand the work of God in salvation, so that a child can grasp it, and the most complex, so that no theologian can ever exhaust its meaning. When Paul wrote of the *'unsearchable riches'* or *'boundless riches'* of Christ (Ephesians 3:8) he was referring above all to the grace of God expressed in the cross. It is a truth that, like being in a forest, the image behind his use of 'unsearchable' leads to endless exploration, even if not all of it is profitable, so the cross is territory we can never cover in its entirety. It is a truth that can never be adequately contained in a neat formula, understood by a simple definition or reduced to a repetitive slogan.

The cross as a simple declaration

Some writing about the cross in the New Testament consists of a straightforward declaration without explanation. It is the assertion of the simple fact that *'the Son of God loved me and gave himself for me'* (Galatians 2:20), or that *'while we were still sinners, Christ died for us'* (Romans 5:8), or that *'we believe that Jesus died and rose again'* (1 Thessalonians 4:14), or that *'he died for us…so that we might live together with him'* (1 Thessalonians 5:10). In a few short words it explains why the death of this man was so special and differs from the multitude of other shame-filled executions which were carried out by the Romans at the time. He was the Son of God, his

---

[2] A Skevington Wood, *The Burning Heart, John Wesley, Evangelist,* Exeter: Paternoster Press, 1967, p. 236.

death was an expression of God's love towards rebellious creatures, and the means by which he chose to forgive sin. The simple declaration, of course, cloaks depths of understanding which draw on a shared heritage in terms of the sacrificial faith of Israel and the ways by which God has chosen to put the world – the world of the Gentiles as well as of the Jews – to rights.

Nonetheless, these and other texts are simple declarations of a historical fact as well as minimalist coded theological assertions that *'Christ died for our sins'* (1 Corinthians 15:3). In a world which is ignorant of the Christian faith, perhaps our first urgent task is to announce the event that lies at the heart of the faith, so that people become aware that Christianity is neither a historical fiction nor a philosophical theory without a foundation. As Dorothy L Sayers wrote,

> He (Jesus) is the only God who has a date in history....There is no more astonishing collocation of phrases than that which, in the Nicene Creed, sets these two statements flatly side by side: 'Very God of Very God...He suffered under Pontus Pilate.' All over the world, thousands of times a day, Christians recite the name of a rather undistinguished Roman proconsul...merely because that name fixes within a few years the date and the death of God.[3]

But we must not be content with the simple declaration that Christ died for our sins. We must strive to understand it for, in P. T. Forsyth's words, 'You do not understand Christ until you understand his cross.'[4]

---

[3] Cited by Philip Yancey, *The Jesus I Never Knew*, London: Marshall Pickering, 1995, p. 200.
[4] P. T. Forsyth, *The Cruciality of the Cross*, Carlisle: Paternoster Press, 1997 (org. ed. 1909) p. 26.

What is expository preaching?

Expository preaching is preaching that involves a three-fold movement. Firstly it involves an announcement: the announcement, in this case, that Christ died for our sins. The announcement is an announcement of what God has revealed in Christ, as recorded in Scripture. There is no need to drive any wedge between the living word of God and the written word of God, as some are keen to do. Expository preaching is biblical preaching and involves a theological commitment about the nature and inspiration of Scripture as well as the person of Christ, at the same time as seeking to allow the biblical text to discipline its contents.

Secondly, it involves, as its very name implies, an exposition. It takes a passage in the Bible where the announcement is made and examines and explains it. The passage is selected with care, so that it is not wrenched out of its context. Decisions about where the unity starts and finishes are made with integrity. In John Stott's inimitable words:

> The expositor prizes open what appears to be closed, makes plain what is obscure, unravels what is knotted, and unfolds that which is tightly packed. The opposite of exposition is 'imposition', which is to impose on the text what is not there.[5]

There may be other forms of preaching, but it is the regular exposition of God's communication to us in the Bible that builds the church and adequately addresses the world. Too much preaching is of a shallow, 'blessed thought' variety which reads into Scripture, if it uses Scripture at all, some imaginative idea but misses out on the obvious truth we are meant to be unfolding.

---

[5] John Stott, *I Believe in Preaching,* London: Hodders, 1982, p. 126.

The third movement is that of application. Expository preaching is neither a verse-by-verse commentary nor a theological lecture. Though shaped and disciplined by the biblical text, the task of expository preaching is incomplete unless the message is applied to the contemporary audience. Exegetical preaching confines itself to an annotation of the text. Expository preaching is exegesis plus application.

The cross as a many-sided wonder

When it comes to the cross, we have plenty of material to serve as the subject of our expository preaching, since the New Testament does far more than announce the death of Christ; it explores and explains it from many different angles.

In the gospels

At first sight, the Gospel writers are content to report the events of the crucifixion and leave it at that. And that is essentially correct. They all reflect on the same event with many of the details being reported identically. However, one is immediately struck on reading the accounts not only by the similarities but also by some differences between them. While traditionally evangelicals have sought to harmonise the accounts, especially perhaps in giving attention to the different chronology which John's Gospel reports in relation to the Synoptic Gospels, a greater appreciation has been shown in recent years of their differences. While, on the surface, the Gospels are primarily telling us about the events of the life, death and resurrection of Jesus they are not doing so in a theological vacuum.

While great care has to be exercised to avoid reading too much into the supposed audiences to which the gospels were originally written and whilst undoubtedly some theologians have taken flights of fantasy in this regard, it is, I think, uncontroversial to claim that each 'author' brings his own doctrinal emphases and theological agenda, not to say literary skill, to his writings because he has a particular readership in view, which he seeks to address. This leads each of them to express things differently and to select different details in relaying the story.

Concerned to present Christ as the King of the Jews and as the fulfilment of Scripture, Matthew's eye is caught by elements which stress his innocence, power and the fulfilment motif which has run throughout the gospel[6]: like Judas betraying Jesus for thirty pieces of silver and then buying a field, the temple curtain being torn in two, the earth shaking as if being re-created, tombs being opened with 'the righteous' being resurrected and the awesomeness experienced by the soldiers guarding his tomb, as one might expect when a King was making his presence felt.

Shorn of the great teaching sections of Matthew and stories of Luke, the cross dominates Mark's gospel. For Mark, possibly written to encourage robust discipleship among those suffering for the faith, it is the conflict motif and bleakness of the scene which strikes one. Because his narrative is lean, the darkness and despair seem more prominent. Like Matthew, he records the cry of desertion but his more concise narrative means that it achieves a new importance. Yet, he also records the confession of the Roman centurion that Jesus was 'surely' the Son of God - a confession which would have been especially relevant if Mark's gospel was written to believers in Rome to encourage them to be robust disciples in the face of

---

[6] See Morna Hooker, *Not Ashamed of the Gospel: The New Testament Interpretations of the Death of Christ,* The Didsbury Lectures. Carlisle: Paternoster, 1994, pp. 68-77. Hooker rightly notes that while the cross is the climax of the fulfilment theme, intriguingly, she does not particularly quote any OT texts in recording the crucifixion itself.

persecution. Here is a powerful Christ who conquers Satan and darkness through suffering.

Luke, the great story teller, presents, in line with the rest of his gospel, a Jesus who is compassionate to the very end. Starting with the restoration of Malchus' severed ear, continuing with expressing concern for the women who witnessed his death march, and then his praying for the forgiveness (another of Luke's major themes) for those who crucified him, it concludes with Jesus' welcoming the dying thief into paradise. Luke does not mention his sense of being deserted by God, but only that, as a trusting son, he commended his spirit to his Father[7] and has full confidence in his Father's ways.

With John we enter a different world of deep reflection, long after the events had occurred. The gospel is arranged according to its literary objectives, rather than strict chronology and the cross is presented as the dying of the lamb of God who takes away the sin of the world, first mentioned in 1:29. The timing of the crucifixion and the details about the hyssop plant and no bones being broken all highlight Jesus as the Passover Lamb, while the trial before Pilate, his carrying his own cross and the indictment above the cross, 'The King of the Jews', teach that this lamb is the lamb who conquers and reigns.[8] In Forsyth's words, although he does not apply them specifically to John, 'He went to death as a king. It was the supreme exercise of his royal self-disposal.'[9] Maintaining the use of paradox to the end, the cross of shame becomes the throne of glory. 'Indeed,' as Morna Hooker stated, 'there is a sense in which John does not contain a "passion" narrative, and

---

[7] Quoting Psalm. 31:5.
[8] In the terms of Revelation 5:5-6, it is 'the Lion of the tribe of Judah' who is the lamb.
[9] Forsyth, p. 38.

it might be truer to describe his account as a "glory" narrative.'[10]

The four accounts give us a fuller view of the cross than anyone could do on its own. As one of my former colleagues used to say when explaining why we have four gospels not one, 'because four gospel are needed to tell the story. One would not be enough.' It is as if each gospel writer views the events of Golgotha from a different vantage point – one from the north, one from the south, one from the east and one from the west. It is not then, either surprising or troubling that they pick out different features. Indeed, it would be troubling if they did not do so.

Scratch beneath the surface and you quickly discover more than 'a mere report of the facts', as if such a thing were ever possible. In the gospels you soon discover a portrait of Jesus as the suffering Messiah, powerful king, compassionate saviour, and Passover lamb. The meaning is inherent in the way the events are told.

In the letters

Nonetheless, it is true that it is in the New Testament letters that the significance of the death of Christ is expounded in depth. Tom Wright has explained that the New Testament is 'a twofold work' consisting of 'first, the Messiah's work; second the apostolic ministry through which the work is put into operation'.[11] Or we might say that Part I primarily emphasises the events and Part II emphasises their interpretation, although as we have seen, this contrast should not be overdrawn.

---

[10] Hooker, p. 109.
[11] N. T. Wright, *Paul and the Faithfulness of God,* Part III, London: SPCK, 2013, p. 880.

Referring to it, the New Testament writers speak of the death of Christ, or of him being crucified, or the crucifixion, rather more than they do of 'the cross'. Whatever language is used, *that Christ died for our sins, according to the Scriptures'* was *'of first importance'* (1 Corinthians 15:3) to Paul and the other New Testament writers, whose writings are permeated with rich and diverse teaching about the cross.

They present the one who died on the cross through the use of images which draw on the wells of Jewish spirituality, such as the sacrificial lamb, the scapegoat, the Passover lamb, the deliverer, the burden-bearer, the substitute, the righteous one, the covenant fulfiller, as well using titles to describe him, like the Son of God, the son of David, the Christ (Messiah), the Lord and the servant. If the one who died under Pontus Pilate was no-one out of the ordinary, his death, at most, would have been an example of self-giving love, or the death of a martyr to a cause, but nothing more. It is only because of whose death it is that we can proclaim the cross as the means of our salvation.

Something objective occurred through the cross of Jesus, the Messiah. Something changed through that cross. God was not simply making his appeal to a wayward humanity to return to him in repentance but making it possible for us to do so because the obstacles that stood in the way of our reconciliation, that is our sin and our captivity under the rule of Satan, was dealt with, once and for all.

As James Denney complained, 'there is much preaching *about* Christ's death which fails to be a preaching of Christ's death'. He wrote that if he was sitting on the end of a pier and someone jumped in the water and drowned '"to prove his love for me" I should find it quite unintelligible.' But if I had fallen off the pier and was drowning and someone drowned in the act of rescuing me I would find that 'intelligible' and say, "'Greater love hath no man than this.'"[12] Christ's death was a death that was necessary because of my sinful state and a death that rescued me from drowning in that sin.

The apostles write in a multitude of ways about the cross with some, like Hebrews, having a particular take on the meaning of his death because of their background and the audience to which they were writing. Paul adjusts his exposition of the cross to the need of his readers. Hence to those who were wondering how many Jewish customs one had to continue to practise to be put right with God, he writes in terms of justification, notably in Romans and Galatians. But to the warring factions of the Corinthian church he writes of the cross in terms of it being the antithesis of power and wisdom of the world that leads to pride and division, and presents it positively as effecting reconciliation. To the churches in Ephesus and Colossae, where believers felt oppressed by destructive spiritual powers and laws, he writes of the cross as a powerful instrument through which God has conquered evil and is putting the world back into a harmonious state under his rule.

While there are individual emphases, together these early preachers press a wide range of images into service to explain the effect of the cross for us and they interject them frequently in their writings. Using images from all over their world and raiding their own experience, they speak of the cross as obtaining:

- ➢ justification for the unjustifiable (the law courts), Romans 3:21-31; 5:9
- ➢ redemption for the captive (the slave market), Ephesians 1:7-14; Colossians 1:14; 1 Peter 1:18-19

---

[12] James Denney, *The Death of Christ,* London: Tyndale Press, 1951, p. 103.

- reconciliation[13] for the alienated (family and friends), Romans 5:8-11; 2 Corinthians 5:11-21; Colossians 1:20
- ransom for the hostage (the victims), Mark 10:45; Hebrews 9:15
- peace for warring factions (the battlefield), Ephesians 2:11-22; Colossians 1:20
- adoption for the orphan (the family), Galatians 3:23-4:7; Ephesians 1:4-8
- healing for the sick (the hospital), Matthew 8:17; 1 Peter 2:24
- regeneration for the dead (the cemetery), 2 Corinthians 5:11-17; Ephesians 2:1-6;
- freedom from oppressing powers (the demonic), Colossians 2:14-15; Hebrews 2:14-15.
- cleansing for the dirty (the temple), Hebrews 9:11-14
- obedience for the disobedient (the covenant), Hebrews 9:15-10:18
- relief for the burdened (like burden-bearing animals), 1 Peter 2:24. [14]

---

[13] Several have recently argued that reconciliation is 'the heart of Paul's missionary theology', partly, one suspects, as a reaction to the traditional evangelical emphasis on justification. Most recently see, Stanley Porter, 'Reconciliation as the heart of Paul's Missionary Theology' in Trevor J. Burke and Brian S. Rosner (eds.) *Paul as Missionary,* London: T & T Clark, 2011, pp. 169-179. John Stott suggested that reconciliation was the most popular image 'because it is the most personal', John Stott, *The Cross of Christ,* Leicester: IVP, 1986, p. 192.

[14] See Brenda B. Colijn, *Images of Salvation in the New Testament,* Downers Grove, IVP Academic, 2010 and Derek Tidball, *Voices of the New Testament*, London: IVP and Downers Grove, IVP Academic, 2016, pp. 146-165. In a standard text, John McIntyre identified thirteen models of 'soteriology', some of which were more explanatory theories than metaphors of salvation. See *the Shape of Soteriology,* Edinburgh: T & T Clark, 1992, ch. 2.

These, and more, are all attempts to present the manifold message of salvation[15] which is accomplished through the cross. The open-endedness of the images of salvation probably set a precedent for us to develop our own contemporary models of salvation. But if we are to do so, we must be careful not to trivialise the salvation that was won through the cross. So, for example, at the height of the drug-fuelled 1960s' counter-culture, it was not uncommon to hear people being invited to 'get high on Jesus'. But whether the experience of a drug-induced ecstasy and the experience of salvation in Christ are truly comparable is extremely doubtful!

Some years ago, Leon Morris, the doyen of evangelical theologians of the atonement, having written a rigorous academic defence of penal substitution, then wrote a little book on the cross of Jesus in which he expounded the cross as the answer to futility, ignorance, loneliness, sickness, death and selfishness.[16] It is a model of how expounding the cross can be applied relevantly to the needs of our contemporary world. In a world of terrorism and hostages, of debts, of dependencies, of broken relationships, of violence and civil war, of failure and guilt, and, yes, where many feel shame, both the need for and the illustrations of salvation abound.

None of the writers were *'ashamed of the gospel'* (Romans 1:16) at the heart of which is the cross of Christ and yet all of them are aware how absurd the message must have sounded to the world to which they spoke. That God should put the world back to rights through the crucifixion of the Messiah was both absurd and offensive, especially since he was a backwoods Jew from the margins of the empire rather than the centre of power. How on earth could people possibly believe it? People looked

---

[15] For an excellent introduction to the wider concept of salvation see, Joel B. Green, *Why Salvation?* Nashville: Abingdon, 2013.
[16] Leon Morris, *The Cross of Jesus*, Grand Rapids: Eerdmans and Exeter: Paternoster, 1988.

for far more sophisticated solutions to the world's problems than a crucified nobody from Nazareth, as Paul admits in 1 Corinthians 1:18-25. Morna Hooker insightfully commented,

> Our problem is simply that we are too used to the Christian story; it is difficult for us to grasp the absurdity – indeed, the sheer madness – of the gospel about a crucified saviour which was proclaimed by the first Christians in a world where the cross was the most barbaric form of punishment which men could devise.[17]

No one in their right minds would have invented a crazy story like this. Yet they proclaimed the message boldly and without embarrassment. Why should we think the task will prove any easier? While we strive to make the message of the cross as intelligible as we can, we know that such a message will always be dismissed as ludicrous and even, in fact, as an obstacle – a stumbling block – to belief since it seems so primitive and illogical to post-enlightenment minds. Let people say we are out of our minds, if they will, but, like Paul, *'Christ's love compels us'* (2 Corinthians 5:14) and we are so convinced of the message that we cannot keep silent.

In later theology

To modern minds, the theology of the New Testament does not quite go far enough as it never explains to their satisfaction why the cross was God's chosen means of salvation and how it was that through the cross sins could be forgiven and salvation achieved. Theologians, then, have developed various models or theories about the cross by which they seek to explain what was happening there. Morna Hooker put the problem like this.

---

[17] Hooker, p. 8.

'the problem lies in the word "for" in the statement "Christ died for our sins." What does "for" mean?'[18]

The historical explanations largely coalesce around four ideas, each of which owe something to the culture in which they were conceived, although that does not determine either their validity or on-going usefulness.

Firstly, there are models that stress the idea that on the cross Jesus satisfied the demands of a holy God. First proposed by Anselm in the 11th century, God is viewed as a sovereign ruler whose honour has been offended by his subjects' disobedience and who demands that satisfaction be made. However, human beings are unable to make sufficient satisfaction, which only a person of 'infinite goodness' can do. The solution was that God should become a man and himself pay the debt which was owed through the cross of his son Jesus. In this way God's honour is satisfied and men and women may be forgiven. He rejects the idea of *penal* substitution, for it is God's honour not his law and justice, which is at stake. Later versions have adjusted details and the model still has currency in some circles.

Secondly, there are models that emphasise the idea that on the cross Jesus was a substitute paying the penalty for our sin. This model emphasises that God is a law-giver and that people are sinners who have broken his law. The problem, then, is how to deal with their guilt and declare them 'justified'. Once again, it is argued that it is impossible for human beings to pay their debt by their own righteousness. It is only possible for the guilty to be set free if someone else who is worthy of doing so (and therefore free from the debt of guilt themselves) pays the penalty on their behalf. Based on verses like Romans 6:23, *'The wages of sin is death, but the gift of God is eternal life*

---

[18] Hooker, p. 7.

through Christ Jesus our Lord.', this model has both biblical roots and a long history. Penal substitution was the primary model taught by the later Reformers and subsequent evangelicals. John Wesley espoused it 'not as a theological theory, but as a plain truth of Scripture.'[19]

In recent days it has been subject to much criticism with the penal element being called into question even when the substitutionary element may be accepted (although not all accept even this and some think it is immoral). It is easy to caricature as an angry father taking it out on a victimised son. But this is a gross distortion and unnecessary misrepresentation of the theory which deserves to be better presented. In his classic work, *The Cross of Christ*, John Stott has, among others,[20] mounted a serious defence of the model in recent years and argued that the cross speaks not of a divided Trinity, with the Father and Son in conflict with each other, but the 'self-substitution of God' and the only way ultimately in which God expresses 'simultaneously his holiness in judgement and his love in pardon.'[21] Attempts to marginalise (or even do away with) penal substitutionary atonement often reflect contemporary, changing views of law and punishment and a softening of the horror of sin rather than being built on an adequate biblical foundation. People, it is said, no longer feel guilty and therefore the model does not communicate to contemporary men and women. Some say, the greater negative emotion people experience, not only in the western world but perhaps especially in the Asian world, is shame, rather than guilt, and that the cross is better explained as Christ bearing

---

[19] Wood, p. 237. Wesley also accepted other models.
[20] A classic recent statement is found in J. I. Packer, 'What Did the Cross Achieve?' in *Celebrating the Saving Work of God,* The Collected Shorter Writings of J. I. Packer, Vol. 1; Carlisle: Paternoster Press, 1998, pp. 85-123. See also I Howard Marshall, *Aspects of the Atonement,* London: Paternoster, 2007.
[21] Stott, *Cross of Christ,* p. 134.

our shame, rather than our guilt, and carrying it away on the cross.[22]

The penal substitutionary view of the cross is closely associated with ideas of sacrifice, atonement and propitiation, such as are found in Romans 3:25; Hebrews 10:1-15; 1 John 2:2; 4:10.

Thirdly, there are models that view the cross essentially as the place where Christ triumphed over God's enemies (and therefore the enemies of humanity too) not by engaging them with violence but by voluntarily surrendering himself to their onslaught. Often referred to as the classic view it was undoubtedly held by the early church fathers, alongside other models, and adopted by Martin Luther, and then gained fresh currency through the writing of Gustav Aulén in his book *Christus Victor* (Christ the Victor) in 1930. Again, the model is found in Scripture in passages like Colossians 2:14-15 and Hebrews 2:14-15. The view especially resonates with those of a pacifist disposition since God conquers his opponent(s) not by using their weapons of violence but by laying down the use of force. The view particularly appeals to those who feel themselves oppressed and in need of a champion who can deliver them.

Fourthly, there are models that view the cross chiefly as an expression of God's love and the appeal he makes to his creatures who are alienated from him to return. This view is often traced back to Abelard, Anselm's younger contemporary in the 11-12th Century. The barrier which needed to be overcome, he argued, is not that of God's holiness but of man's reluctance. It is often known as the moral influence theory.

---

[22] See, for example, Joel B. Green & Mark D. Baker, *Recovering the Scandal of the Cross, Atonement in the New Testament & Contemporary Contexts,* Downers Grove, IVP, 2000, and Alan Mann, *Atonement for a 'Sinless' Society: Engaging with an Emerging Culture,* Milton Keynes, Paternoster, 2005.

While the cross is undoubtedly an expression of God's love (1 John 3:16) and presented as exemplary (Philippians 2:5-11 and 1 Peter 2:21-25) it is grossly inadequate to reduce our understanding of the cross to it being merely an expression of his love to which we should respond and which we are called to imitate. It is not less than that, but it is so much more than that. An exemplary death is never going to provide an adequate salvation, since as sinful human beings perfectly matching the example it sets is impossible for us. The cross must do something, it must change something between a sinful humanity and a holy God, or Christ is not an adequate saviour and as Paul said, albeit about the necessity of the resurrection, without it, *'your faith is futile and you are still in our sins'* (1 Corinthians 15:17).

These models can help to illuminate aspects of the theology of the crucifixion and yet, as preachers, we must be careful not to preach theories but announce certainties. Philip Brooks in his classic lectures on preaching rebuked many in his day like this:

> There are many preachers who seem to do nothing else, always discussing Christianity as a problem instead of announcing Christianity as a message and proclaiming Christ as a Saviour. I do not undervalue their discussions. But I think we ought always to feel that such discussions are not the type or ideal of preaching. They may be necessities of the time, but they are not the work which the great Apostolic preachers did, or which the true preacher will always desire....*Beware the tendency to preach about Christianity rather than to preach Christ.*[23]

---

[23] Philip Brooks, *Lectures on Preaching*, (Delivered to Yale Divinity School) London: Allenson & Co. Ltd, 1877, pp. 20-21. Italics mine.

We are called to be heralds who proclaim, sensitively and meaningfully in our own context, the clear message of what God has done to redeem the world and reconcile people to himself through the death of Christ.

The cross and the contemporary church

I conclude with three further comments.

Firstly, the cross is not only a past event but is also determines the present, daily experience of the disciples of Jesus. He calls them to carry the cross (Matthew 16:24-26; Luke 9:23). The call is not a call to bear an ordinary human burden, like sickness (or one's mother-in-law), but to die to self and to enter into the fellowship of his sufferings (Philippians 3:10). The cross is both an objective, historical act of God and the essential contemporary reality of his disciples. We not only 'survey the wondrous cross' but participate in it. The cross, then, is not only about our initial conversion but our on-going sanctification. Preachers who do not carry the cross personally cannot hope to be effective or be seen as authentic.

Secondly, the call to carry the cross is not only a call for the individual preacher but a call to the church corporately. The cross, then, is about our ecclesiology as much as our personal atonement. Our churches should be cruciform in shape, not architecturally, but in life-style, sacrificial service and mutual submission. That was the call to the church in Corinth after Paul expounded the weakness and folly of the cross in 1 Corinthians 1:18-25 and that call to self-denial permeates the teaching of the New Testament about the church. It is sadly a long way from the way in which many behave within our churches today who seem devoid of a basic understanding of the foundation of their faith. The cross, not culture, is to be the most powerful influence shaping our corporate lives.

Thirdly, as we preach the cross, we must not only announce it and expound its meaning, but must appeal to people to respond to the wonderful offer of salvation which flows from it. Donald English wisely warned of the need to ensure we keep the delicate balance between the quality of the meal we offer people and the invitation to all to sit down and eat.

> There is a kind of preacher whose theological weight is such that you are constantly told about a wonderful banquet, but never invited to the table or told how to get there. There is another kind that constantly and urgently invites you to the table and tells you how to come, without giving you any sense that what is on the table is worth the journey! Our hearers need a theological content that whets their appetite and a faith content that enables them to enter fully into all that God can be for their lives.[24]

Summary

Our message has not changed and we are called in our day to 'boast in, glory in, trust in, rejoice in, revel in and live for'[25] the cross of Christ, as Paul says he himself did in Galatians 6:14. It should be our only obsession, relegating all other passions lower down our agendas. It is an inexhaustible message which will keep us going until our dying day. As I wrote some time ago:

> At Calvary, sin is forgiven, atonement is made, the guilty are pardoned, enemies are reconciled, alienation is overcome, friendship is restored, freedom is purchased, salvation is won, grace is bestowed, peace is proffered,

---

[24] Donald English, *An Evangelical Theology of Preaching*, Nashville: Abingdon, 1996, pp. 64-65.
[25] Stott, *Cross of Christ*, p. 349.

lives are transformed, Satan is disarmed, rebirth is conceivable, a new age is inaugurated and cosmic renewal is begun - and much more beside.[26]

That should be enough to lay to rest for ever that preaching the message of the cross will lead to a hollow, repetitive preaching of a simple slogan. There will always be a way to present this message so as to match the needs of individuals and communities, for it is the best news of all and God's only solution for sin-sick lives.

---

[26] *LBC Review,* 'The Cross, reflections and resources' 2011.

For further reading:

The literature on atonement is voluminous but these are selected particularly with evangelical preachers in mind.

Morna Hooker, *Not Ashamed of the Gospel: The New Testament Interpretations of the Death of Christ*, The Didsbury Lectures. Carlisle: Paternoster, 1994.

I Howard Marshall, *Aspects of the Atonement*, London: Paternoster, 2007.

Tom Smail, *Once and for All: A Confession of the Cross*, London: Darton, Longman and Todd, 1998.

John Stott, *The Cross of Christ*, Leicester: IVP, 1986.

Derek Tidball, *The Message of the Cross*, The Bible Speaks Today, Leicester, IVP, 2001.